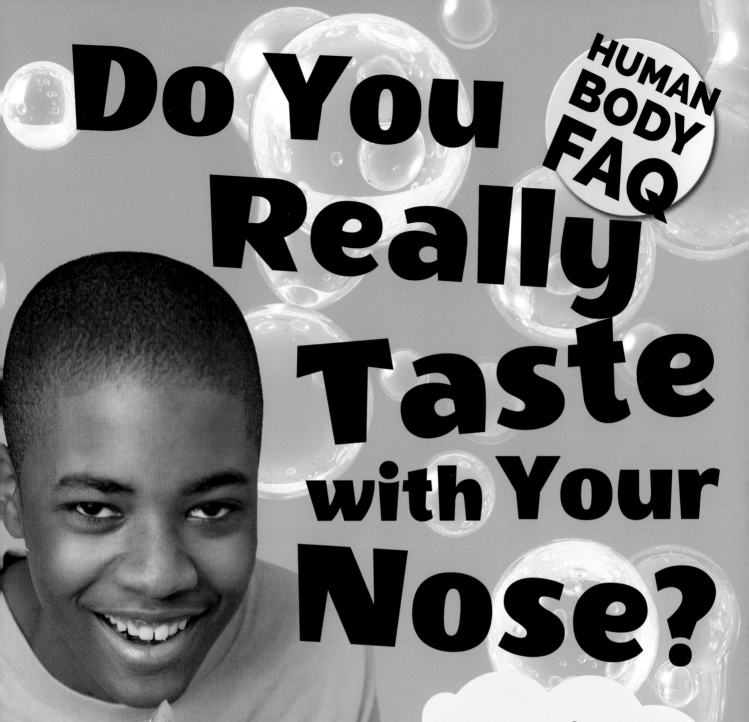

Do You Really Taste with Your Nose?

HUMAN BODY FAQ

Questions About the Senses

by **Thomas Canavan**

PowerKiDS
press

Published in 2017 by **The Rosen Publishing Group, Inc.**
29 East 21st Street, New York, NY 10010

Cataloging-in-Publication Data
Names: Canavan, Thomas.
Title: Do you really taste with your nose? / Thomas Canavan.
Description: New York : PowerKids Press, 2017. | Series: Human body FAQ | Includes index.
Identifiers: ISBN 9781499431636 (pbk.) | ISBN 9781499432213 (library bound) |
  ISBN 9781499431643 (6 pack)
Subjects: LCSH: Senses and sensation--Juvenile literature.
Classification: LCC QP434.C317 2017 | DDC 612.8--dc23

Author: Thomas Canavan
Designers: Supriya Sahai and Emma Randall
Editors: Joe Harris and Anna Brett
Cover design: Paul Oakley

Cover illustration: Shutterstock
Interior illustrations: Shutterstock

Manufactured in the United States of America
CPSIA Compliance Information: Batch #BW17PK: For Further Information contact Rosen Publishing, New York, New York at 1-800-237-9932.

Contents

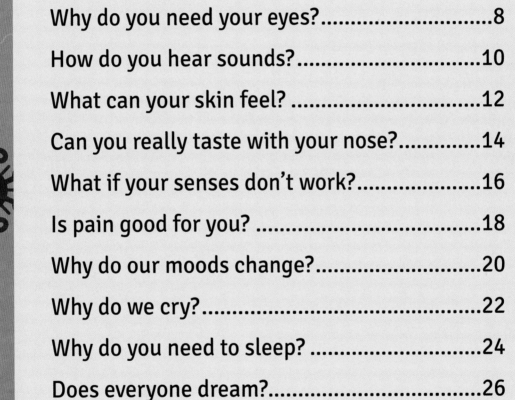

How busy is your brain?

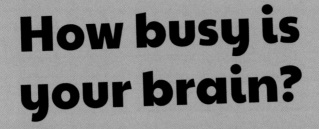

Think of everything that's going on around you right now. Even while you're concentrating on thinking about it, thousands of other things are happening, both around you and inside your body. Luckily your brain can make sense of it all, and avoid total confusion.

Does your brain need exercise?

Yes! Doctors recommend reading, playing musical instruments, and doing puzzles as ways of keeping the brain "fit" well into old age.

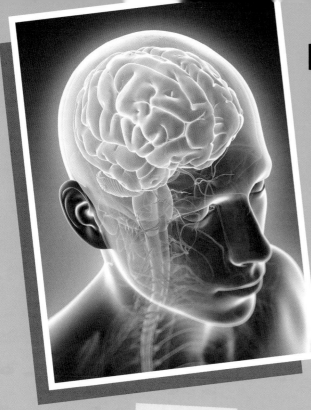

Does your brain work like a computer?

In many ways your brain is like a computer, constantly analyzing data and acting on that stimulation. But even the most advanced computer can't match the brain in quickly sending information back along its own system. The most powerful computer is still 30 times slower than your brain!

How big is the human brain?

An adult brain weighs around 3.3 pounds (1.5 kg)—about the same as a medium oven-ready chicken. It measures about 6 inches (15 cm) long.

Do we notice everything around us?

We often focus on one thing and ignore other activities. It's called selective attention. In one experiment, scientists ask viewers to count how often a group of basketball players pass the ball in a short video clip. People concentrate on counting, but often miss the man in a gorilla costume that walks through the group of players!

No monkey business!

5

How do messages reach your brain?

Your senses pick up messages from the outside world, but they need the brain to make sense of them. Messages travel around your body via a network of nerves that together make up the nervous system. Nerves work like roads for messages to travel along. However, there are never any traffic jams, as messages travel around the body at speeds of up to 250 mph (400 km/h)!

Can you ignore messages from your senses?

You can't choose whether or not messages from your nervous system reach the brain. However, you can usually choose how to react to them. For example, if you receive a message saying that you've encountered a bad smell, you can make the decision to hold your nose!

What is a reflex action?

A reflex action is an extra-fast response from your nervous system that doesn't involve your brain at all. The message travels through your nerves in a loop called a "reflex arc." Doctors can check your reflex actions by gently tapping your kneecap. The message from your knee only travels as far as your spine before a response is sent back and your leg kicks out!

Why are some people better at catching?

To catch a ball, a message from your eyes has to travel to your brain and the brain has to instruct your hands how to move. This takes time, but the more you practice, the more your brain will get used to receiving and sending the same message.

Why are some areas of the body more sensitive than others?

Some parts of the body have more nerve endings than others, as they pick up more messages from the outside world. If your body grew in proportion to the number of nerve endings you have, you'd look like this man! Your hands, lips and mouth would all be huge to account for all those nerves.

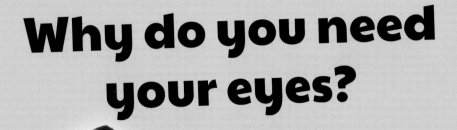

Why do you need your eyes?

Sight is one of the most important human senses, and saying "I see" in many languages means "I understand." Your eyes do an excellent job of observing what's happening around you and sending that information to your brain. Sight is so important that around half of your brain is involved in seeing. But sometimes even these precision tools need adjusting.

What happens when we see double?

If your eyes aren't looking in exactly the same direction, your brain can't form a single, 3-D image so you see two images.

Why do we have two eyes?

Light and images pass through your eye and reach the retina, where they're turned into electrical signals and sent off to the brain. One eye could do this job well, but it wouldn't be able to help you judge depth, or distance. The brain judges the slightly different images from the two eyes and works out how far away objects are.

Are both your eyes always the same?
Not always. Some children develop a "lazy eye" which sees less clearly than the other eye.

How do eyeglasses help people see?

Images pass through lenses (curved, clear bits of tissue) on your eyes on the way to the retinas. Sometimes the lenses lose their shape and no longer send clear images—like an out-of-focus photograph. Eyeglasses have special lenses to correct these problems.

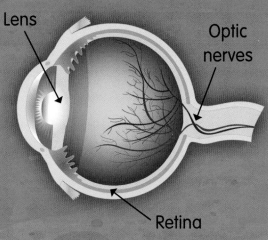

Lens

Optic nerves

Retina

How do you hear sounds?

Sounds are made by vibrations that create waves which pass through the air and are captured by our ears. It's the ears' job to turn those air vibrations into electrical signals that get sent to the brain. Like a radio receiving its signals, the brain transforms those into the sounds we hear.

Can loud noises hurt you?

Very loud noises can kill cells in the inner ear, so over time, if enough of these cells die, a person can suffer from hearing loss.

Do your ears make you seasick?

The inner ear has two jobs. One is to translate vibrations into electrical sound signals. The other is to help your sense of balance. Your brain analyzes fluid inside your inner ear to keep you upright and balanced. You can get seasick if the information from this fluid level doesn't match the information sent from your eyes.

It's all about the balance...

Is it possible to have complete silence?

Not really... even inside soundproof containers, people still hear the hums, thumps, and buzzes of their own heart and nerves.

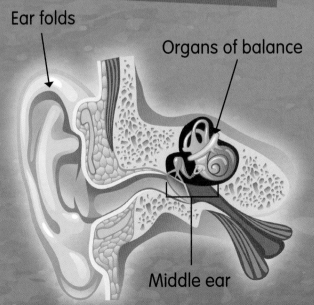

Ear folds

Organs of balance

Middle ear

Why do ears have those folds of skin?

Those folds act like a funnel, trapping sound waves and sending them into your ear even more strongly. The waves cause tiny bones in your middle ear to vibrate. And those vibrations cause even tinier cells in your inner ear to send electrical signals to the brain, which registers them as sounds.

What can your skin feel?

Ouch!

In case you've forgotten, your skin is your body's largest organ. It has many jobs to do, apart from protecting what's inside it. One of the most important is to send signals from its receptors—which are sensitive to heat, cold, and pressure—to the brain. It's your sense of touch.

Why do I "burn" my tongue?

Your tongue is sensitive to pain and pressure, but it is not so sensitive to heat. Sometimes, we drink things that are too hot, but we don't realize until our tongue is already "burned."

Why are some parts of your body more sensitive?

The skin is packed with nerve endings, known as sensors, which pick up signals and send them on to the brain. Specialized sensors detect pressure, heat, cold, pain, and itches. Some parts of your body, such as your fingertips and face, are loaded with sensors. Others, such as your back and belly, have fewer sensors, and so are less sensitive.

How do people read by touch?

Many blind people can use their fingers to follow patterns of raised dots on a page, using the Braille writing system.

What happens when we're tickled?

The nerve signals from a light touch pass near the part of the brain that detects pleasure. That's why we usually laugh when we're tickled. But the brain also filters out unimportant information. So if you try to tickle yourself, your brain isn't fooled and it ignores the urge to laugh.

Can you really taste with your nose?

Does your mouth water when you smell a lasagna cooking in the oven? And do you find that you can't taste food when your head is stuffed up with a cold? These are examples of how your nose and mouth act as a team to guide your sense of taste.

Do women have a better sense of smell than men?

Tests suggest that women do, but the reason might be linked to practice—they usually use their sense of smell more actively than men do.

How many different tastes can we detect?

Every food has dissolved molecules that taste buds in your tongue can detect. They send signals to your brain when they pick up one of the main taste sensations: sweet, sour, salty, bitter, and umami (a strong taste in tomatoes, soy sauce, some cheeses, and cooked meats).

YUCK!

Durian fruit

How much difference does smell make?

You might be surprised to learn that nearly three-quarters of what you taste comes from your sense of smell. Your nose detects molecules that give each object its special smell. It sends those signals to the brain, which also picks up the basic taste signals. Without smell, you couldn't distinguish between two different sour, or salty, foods.

What is the worst-smelling food?
One of the most common answers is the Asian fruit known as durian—it smells so bad that it is banned on many buses and trains.

What if your senses don't work?

Some people are born without one of their senses. In other people, a sense such as hearing may get worse with age. The human body is very good at adapting, so if one of your senses doesn't work, you won't necessarily be at a disadvantage. Your other senses may even work harder. Look at how blind Paralympic athletes are still able to compete at the top level.

Can you "see" by hearing?

Some blind people use their sense of hearing to help them move around. They make clicking sounds and listen to the echoes of the clicks to locate objects around them. It's known as "echolocation."

How do hearing aids work?

A hearing aid has three basic parts – a microphone, an amplifier, and a speaker. The microphone picks up sound waves and converts them to electrical signals. The amplifier increases the power of these signals and the speaker projects them into the inner ear where the vibrations are picked up.

Can you "hear" the color green?

Scientists think that sometimes the neurons in nerves accidentally cross over each other so messages take the wrong pathway. A message from your eyes saying you've seen the color green might be passed to the hearing part of the brain by mistake, making you think you've heard it!

Why does your vision blur if you bump your head?

If you bump the area of your brain that processes the messages from your eyes, then the message from your eyes will arrive, but it won't be processed properly until your brain recovers.

Is pain good for you?

OWWW!

No one likes to feel pain, but without it you'd be in real trouble. That's because pain is the body's alarm system. It's a way of telling you to stop doing something that could be really damaging—like hitting your thumb again with a hammer or walking after you've sprained your ankle.

Is a headache really a pain in your brain?

No. The brain has very few pain receptors so it can't send out pain signals. Most headaches are caused by pain in muscles in your head and neck.

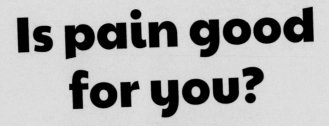

18

Do some people feel no pain?

Some people—luckily very few—are born unable to feel pain. Their nervous system cannot send those essential warning signals to the brain. Occasionally an illness will cause people to lose their sense of pain, and they run the same risks.

Do we really have a funny bone?

What we call the funny bone—that part of your elbow that gives a zinging feeling when you bang it—is actually a nerve rubbing against a bone in your arm.

Does pain always lead you to a problem spot?

It usually does. You can normally tell which toe you've just stubbed or where someone just poked you with their elbow. But pain around the mouth—especially toothache—can be misleading. The network of nerves in your jaw is so tangled that the problem tooth isn't always near the worst pain.

Why do our moods change?

For years, people were undecided how moods and emotions—feeling happy, sad, or afraid—happened. We now know that they're linked to chemical and electrical changes in our bodies. Things like food, sunshine, exercise, and even our pets can produce those changes.

Why do dogs visit hospitals?

Hospital patients feel happier, but also recover faster, if they have a chance to pet a dog or another pet.

How can running make you happy?

Our bodies constantly produce chemicals called hormones that send messages to the rest of the body. Some of these hormones help us fight disease, and others affect our moods. We can become excited, sad, or happy. Exercise releases some positive hormones that can brighten our mood, which is why people sometimes talk about a "runner's high."

Can doctors measure happiness?

They can measure some of the brain activity that occurs when people are happy. Other specialists can help people relax and examine their own feelings and moods. These relaxed discussions are called therapy, and they help people keep a healthy outlook on life.

Why do we cry?

Crying can be a sign of sadness, but your eyes produce tears in other circumstances, too. Some tears are triggered by our feelings, but others are made every day to wash away dust and other things that shouldn't be in our eyes.

Why do newborn babies cry?

The wailing is the first chance that babies have to get oxygen from the air, rather than from their mother's blood. But they don't produce tears until they are a few weeks old.

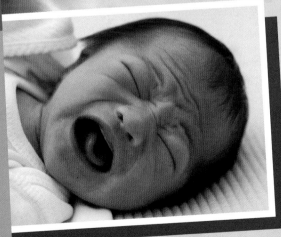

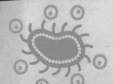

Why does crying make your nose run?

Some tears drain into tiny openings in the eyelids and end up inside your nose. You swallow some but others mix with your nasal fluid, making you sniffly. The excess tears spill down your cheeks.

Is there such a thing as a "good cry"?

Scientists have found that the body produces a natural painkiller when we cry, so perhaps crying really does help.

Boo hoo!

Does crying always mean that we're sad?

Other strong emotions—especially sudden happiness—can also make us cry. And because crying is one of the best ways of rinsing, it helps to defend the eyes against painful particles and smells. Just think of how people cry when they cut onions.

Why do you need to sleep?

You spend hours each night—and sometimes during the day—fast asleep, but what is actually going on in your body? Sleep gives our bodies the chance to rebuild, without being constantly on the go. Your muscles grow, tissue gets repaired, and your body is generally restored. It also gives your mind a chance to process and store information, ready for the next new day.

What is sleepwalking?

Some people sit up in bed and even get up, walk, and talk while they're still asleep, usually within an hour of falling asleep.

24

How long should people sleep?

We need less sleep as we get older—starting with about 16 hours a day for babies and down to about nine hours (teenagers) and eventually less than seven hours. Over an average lifetime, you can spend over 200,000 hours—around 23 years—asleep!

Zzzzz...

What makes us wake up?

The cells in your body need more nutrition and oxygen, and they call on you to become active again—so you can eat, and increase your heart rate.

What happens if you go without sleep?

People suffer if they miss a night's sleep, or if their sleep is constantly interrupted. A person could sleep for more than eight hours, but if that sleep is broken they wake up feeling tired. Prolonged sleepless periods can affect people's moods and their physical and mental health.

Does everyone dream?

We all dream when we're asleep. People who think that they don't have dreams simply can't remember them. Dreaming is part of a cycle that goes on each time we fall asleep. And although we know more about dreams, experts still disagree about why we dream... and what dreams mean.

Can some foods give you nightmares?

Eating late, rather than eating particular foods, can disturb your sleep and lead to the type of nasty dream that might wake you—a nightmare.

Can we tell what dreams mean?

It's easy to tell when we're dreaming—our eyes move quickly, even while they're closed. Many people can remember what they dream. But what the dreams mean is harder to say. People once believed that dreams predicted the future. Doctors now admit that they are mysterious, but perhaps a way of sorting out memories.

How long do dreams last?

Some are only a few seconds long, but others can be up to an hour long.

Nerve impulse in brain

What happens when we dream?

Your nightly sleep follows a pattern, or cycle. Much of that is a deep sleep, when the body rebuilds, but several times during the cycle you pass through a period of Rapid Eye Movement (REM). It reflects how active your brain is, as nerve impulses in your brain play out to form dreams.

How does everything work together?

Our bodies are made up of different systems. Each system has its own function, such as converting food into energy, or removing waste. The systems all work together to bring the human body to life.

Circulatory system

Your heart is at the center of this system, which pumps blood around your body via veins and arteries.

Skeletal system

All 206 bones make up the skeletal system, which supports and protects your body.

Muscular system

Around 640 muscles in your body help you move. Your muscles are attached to your bones by tendons.

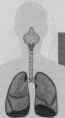

Respiratory system

Your lungs draw in air to bring oxygen into the body and push air out to move carbon dioxide out.

Nervous system

The brain passes messages around the body via a system of nerves. Nerves also pass messages received by your senses back to the brain.

Excretory system

Toxins and waste materials are removed from your body by this system, which includes your kidneys and bladder.

Testes (male)

Digestive system

This system takes in food, and breaks it down into energy and basic nutrients the body can use.

Endocrine system

Glands in this system produce chemicals called hormones that help you grow and change your mood.

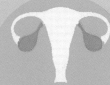

Ovaries (female)

Glossary

Braille A writing system made up of patterns of raised dots that fingers can touch and recognize as letters and words.

cell The smallest functioning unit in an organism. Cells join together to make tissue.

disease A breakdown in the regular function of a part of the body.

echolocation The process of listening to the echo that sounds make off nearby objects.

emotions Feelings such as happiness or anger that are affected by circumstance or mood.

hormone A chemical that helps to regulate processes such as reproduction, growth and blood glucose levels.

inner ear The part of the ear responsible for balance and for converting vibrations into electrical signals for nerves to transmit.

kneecap The bone in front of the knee joint.

molecule The smallest possible unit of a substance that still behaves like that substance. A molecule is made up of two or more atoms.

nerves Fibers in the body that transmit messages around the body.

neuron One of the basic cells of the nervous system.

nightmare A bad dream.

nutrient Any substance that the body needs for energy or growth.

optic nerve The nerve that transports messages from the eyes to the brain.

organ A collection of cells that work together to perform a specific function.

oxygen A colorless, odorless gas found in the air that the body breathes in.

reflex An action performed without conscious thought as response to a stimulus.

retina The area at the back of the eye that passes electrical messages from light sensitive cells to the optic nerve.

stimulation A cause that triggers nervous activity in the body.

tissue A collection of cells that look the same and have a similar job to do in the body.

umami One of the main taste sensations picked up by the tongue.

vitamin A group of molecules that are taken in by the body for nutrition.

Further Information

Further reading

Fundamental Science: My Senses *by Ruth Owen*
(Ruby Tuesday Books Ltd, 2016)

How the Body Works *by editors of DK* (Dorling Kindersley, 2016)

Let's Learn About... The 5 Senses *by Nuria Roca*
(Barron's Educational Series, 2006)

My Little Book About Me *by Angela Royston* (QED Publishing, 2016)

Navigators: Human Body *by Miranda Smith* (Kingfisher, 2015)

Science in Action: Your Brain *by Sally Hewitt* (QED Publishing, 2016)

Websites

PowerKids Press has developed an online list of websites related to the subject of this book. This site is updated regularly. Please use this link to access the list:
www.powerkidslinks.com/hbfaq/nose

Index